Distress

Rudy Bryan Rabemanisa
Andriamampandry

BookLeaf
Publishing

India | USA | UK

Presentation by *BookLeaf Publishing*

Web: www.bookleafpub.com

E-mail: info@bookleafpub.com

ISBN: 978-93-5744-419-4

First edition 2022

Lies

You said I would never lose you
You promised you would always be there

You said I love you
You said you care

You said you would never hurt me

Friend

I may not know much about human relationships
I'm not very bright, I am stupid and ignorant as
you said many times
And I'm not important

But I know that leaving someone behind is an
act of cowardice

Small

You made me feel so small
like a tool you would toss aside when you no
longer need it
So easy to throw away
Worthless

I love you

I love you...

Some people wait for years, for decades, for a
miracle to finally hear those words

And there's you
One day You say I love you
The next day you act like i don't exist
You give then take everything away
That's just cruel

Promises

I will keep all the promises you made
I will cherish them, treasure them for as long as I
live
But It tears me to pieces
It tears me to pieces to know that you never
meant any of them

Red

The sky is burning red
From all the tears I shed

Red screams in the middle of the night
It's cruel how everyday has turned into a fight

Because now,
Everything I see is red
Every person I meet is red
Everything I feel is red

Red...
Red like blood pouring from the fresh wounds of
yesterday and the days before

Red...
You turned everything to red

Shattered

A part of me regrets we ever crossed paths

Another part still believes every word you said

Another part is scared, confused and lost

Another part feels guilty for not being good
enough, for the other parts I cannot change

Another part feels stupid for I lowered my guard
down

And another part will never stop loving you

Gravity

I cannot live without you
Gravity always pulls me back to you
You keep me down,and I can't get up
Gravity,
Makes me care about people that do not care
about me

Begging

I'm kneeling at your feet
Please stop hurting me

Please

Please don't leave
I can't yell any louder
Please stay
Please

Words and scars

words
You can't protect your heart from words
Words can't be taken back
They cut, sink deep
Deeper and deeper
Until it becomes part of your brain
A permanent scar

The reason

You are the reason

The reason why I smile
And the reason why I cry

The reason why I believe I will be okay
The reason why I will never stop hurting

The only reason why believed in love
The only reason why I can't let anyone in
anymore

Coward

I just want you to know
You hurt me
You are cruel
Cold
You're not a good person
You made me believe, then took everything
away from me
You make the rules as you go
And I am never allowed to open my mouth
Now I'm Waiting for an apology that will never
come
You are a Coward

Just in case

Just in case
I love you

Just in case
Goodbye

Last hope

I hate you
I love you
I can't decide which one is worse

You watch me cry
and say nothing

You watch me die
Please say something

Take it back

I just need you to say I love you
And mean it
Or take the I love yous you promised back
Take it back,
Unsay your words
Unbreak my heart

Because of you

Because of you
I am terrified of letting anyone close ever again
Because of you
I am scared of letting people see the broken parts
of me
Because of you
I'm ashamed of my scars, I am I need love to
function
I am ashamed of carrying all this pain
Because of you

Unfair

I Smile
The way I'm supposed to

I smile to please you

But you aren't here now that I need you to make
me smile too

Untitled

I am not crazy
Your hand is on my throat
I explained my wounds and my scars
Only so you won't hurt me too
But you did anyway, over and over and over
again
I don't understand why you do that
And now I am punishing myself for believing in
you

Boomerang

It's not fair that you get to hurt me
Then you get away with it

When someone says you hurt them
You can't just say you didn't
Coz you already did

I am a boomerang
You hurt me, you throw me away
I bleed, but I come back for more
Because I believe in the good in you

But It's not fair
Now I have nowhere to go
Nowhere to return to
A homeless boomerang
It's sad but my heart will keep spinning until it
comes back in your hands

Hoping yet knowning that it will never happen

Infinite

The universe is infinitely big
The universe is infinitely small

What about me? What about us?

Did we even happen?

Noone will know at the end

There is only right now, if you have something
to say
Say it, don't keep it for yourself

If you know someone needs help,help them the
best you can, maybe you are the only who does

I know, what will that change in The infinity of
the universe?

Well, kind words can create universes of their
heart or destroy them
Be careful

I love you can make someone feel infinite
But So does a hurtful word

www.ingramcontent.com/pod-product-compliance
Lightning Source LLC
LaVergne TN
LVHW050309200726